The House Sitters How-to Handbook

Your Complete Guide to Travel & Adventure as a House Sitter

By Rick & Colleen Ray

Copyright 2012

D1511208

For more house sitting adventures follow our blog at

http://www.ouradventureshousesitting.com

This book is dedicated to our

family and our friends.

No matter where in the world we are,

you mean the world to us!

TABLE OF CONTENTS

INTRODUCTION

Are you a traveler waiting to come out of the closet? Are you a travel voyeur who seeks out travel blogs, stays up too late watching the Travel Channel, someone who can't part with those old National Geographic magazines? Do you yearn for the adventure that only comes from experiencing another culture, another country? Or, are you already a traveler and trying to figure out how you can afford your next adventure and the one after that?

Perhaps you are simply looking for a good vacation once in a while or a weekend away, a break from your daily routine. Close to home or further afield, but a trip that isn't going to burn through all of your savings.

Maybe you fantasize about living in another country full or part time? Is International House Hunters your favorite television program? Do you rush to the mailbox to see if your copy of International Living magazine has arrived? Would you like to "try on" some other lifestyles before you make the big move?

If any of this sounds familiar, then house sitting could be the perfect fit for you, just as it has turned out to be for us. We've done the homework, learned a lot along the way, and we've put it all together here to share with you.

In the following chapters we'll tell you everything you need to know to take full advantage of the opportunities that house sitting can offer.

Briefly, this is what we'll cover in each of the chapters:

Chapter 1 — A bit about our experiences and how we came to be house sitters, the benefits and opportunities house sitting provides, and the amazing range of house sits available worldwide.

Chapter 2 — An overview of house sitting and caretaking and their differing expectations, duties, and compensations.

Chapter 3 — Determining your comfort zone as a house sitter with a self-assessment questionnaire that will help guide you in choosing the house sits that best fit you and the homeowner.

Chapter 4 — Finding the perfect house sit including a review of house sitting websites, their services and costs, and some helpful marketing tips.

Chapter 5 — How to create a profile that gets results, a step-by-step guide with example profiles. Suggestions to make the most of the photos you post and linking to social media sites.

Chapter 6 — Putting together all the "extras" you'll need: how to create a strong reference letter library when you've never done a house sit before (including a sample letter), types of police clearance letters and where to obtain them, passports, international driver's permits and how you get one.

Chapter 7 — Landing the assignment you want, working through the selection and interview process step-by-step, and all the things you need to consider before you make a commitment.

Chapter 8 — Preparing for short and long-term assignments, tips on what you'll need for your house sit, security while traveling, and a special section for those considering full time house sitting with a guide and timeline to prepare you for a life on the road.

Chapter 9 — Your first assignment, a guide to everything you need to know about the house and the pets before the homeowner entrusts their care to you with our suggestions for preventing and resolving problems during a house sit.

Chapter 10 — Preparing for the homeowner's return, a review of the steps you need to take before you leave to ensure that you are invited back again.

By the end of chapter 10, you will have all of the information you need to become a successful house sitter. To assist you in that effort we created four helpful forms that you may print for your personal use. These forms can be found at the end of the book and include:

- a contact log for tracking your house sitting applications
- an arrival checklist of each of the items you need to address with the homeowner prior to their departure
- a pet care information form to assist you in collecting all of the necessary data on each pet you will be caring for
- a departure checklist outlining all the steps you need to take before the homeowner returns

Note: If you would like a PDF of these forms sent directly to you, please send us an e-mail request and we will be happy to do so. Our contact information is included at the end of the book.

Before we begin, please note that we generally use the term "house sitting" throughout the book and not "pet sitting" or "caretaking". However, our use is meant to be inclusive of all of the aspects of "house sitting" and the information presented is applicable across the board.

Chapter 1

WHY WE HOUSE SIT AND THINK YOU SHOULD TOO

We are two youthful retirees, ages 54 and 65, that have traveled extensively in the last few years. We loved it so much that we went through a chunk of our savings doing it. We spent money on traveling that we really shouldn't have. But we became addicted. We knew it the day we were sitting in the airport waiting for a flight back home and neither of us wanted to go back. We wanted to wash our clothes, climb on another plane, and go somewhere we'd never been. It wasn't that we didn't like our home or enjoy our life, but something else was calling to us. The romantic thing would be to call it wonder lust. Whatever it was, it was a feeling that wouldn't go away.

We did continue to go home though, trip after trip. But we kept talking about how we could get away more often. We could do house trades, or we could sell our house and all of our belongings, or we could get a house sitter, or we could rent out our house or.... our minds spun around and around, unable to reach a conclusion. Then, while on a trip to Mexico we met a woman who was house sitting and had been for many years. That was how she lived her life. It seemed like something that we could do too. It seemed like the time was right. Were we willing to take the plunge?

Two months later, we were listed on several websites seeking house sitting assignments. We'd done the research, lots of it. We had put together profiles and reference letters, obtained police clearance letters and international driver's permits, and interviewed with homeowners via phone, e-mails and Skype. Our first assignment was all arranged. We'd be in Mexico for seven weeks and a few months after that we had a second assignment lined up in Canada. We hadn't yet filled in the time between the two, but somehow we knew that we would.

All of our belongings were stashed in a 10x30 storage unit, our home was leased out and we were ready to embark upon life on the road, with 2 carry-on suitcases each, two laptops, and a cell phone with an international calling plan. Our bills were all paperless and accessible to pay on-line, what little mail we were expecting was going to a family member. We'd notified banks and credit card companies of our plans, paid our taxes, visited our doctors and dentists for annual physical exams, and stockpiled prescription meds. We did our best to cover all of our bases.

We let all of our friends know what we were doing and spent time with our families, encouraging everyone to get on Skype so we could stay connected. Finally, we were ready to go. We were on a journey without a known ending. We had one-way tickets! We'd done it, we were committed, and we were about to embark upon the biggest adventure of our lives.

Has it been easy? The answer is yes and no. It has taken planning and research and patience. We've had our moments of frustration. We've become more flexible than we knew we could ever be. But we've been rewarded in more ways than we can count.

We've met people whom we never would have crossed paths with in the course of our "old life" who have welcomed us with open arms into their homes and their hearts. People who have trusted us with their beloved pets and most treasured possessions. We've had the enormous pleasure of having pets without being tied to one place as we would be with our own.

We've been introduced to communities and cultures in a way that can only come from time spent living in them and becoming a part of them, albeit temporarily. We've traveled to more places, for longer periods of time, that we thought we ever would. We truly would not trade this experience for anything. As Saint Augustine said, "The world is a book and those that do not travel have read only one page." Through house sitting we've been given the chance to create our own epic novel.

Where in the world will you go? Anywhere you please. House sitting opportunities abound around the world. In a single day, we found these examples of house sits:

"House by the sea in Margaret River, Australia, no pets, garden to water, will provide vehicle..."

"Beautiful post renaissance style castle, 90 minutes by train from Paris, within 10 minute walk of village with all amenities..."

"Ranch in the foothills of southwest New Mexico, 3 dogs need daily walking and 2 cats need lots of TLC..."

"Need someone for off the grid house on the big Island of Hawaii, must be willing to commit to six months or longer..."

"Upscale condo in Washington D.C., near all monuments, need someone to watch my cats for the weekend..."

"Private island on Lake Victoria, Uganda, caretaker needed to provide presence on island..."

"Tend our organic garden in Norway and enjoy our vegetables while you are here. Chickens will provide fresh eggs..."

"Rural farm in Tuscany with small apartment available for one month, must have own transportation..."

"Multi-tasking couple wanted to answer our business phones, feed pets and take care of house and yard on Koh Chang Island, Thailand, while we take a much needed vacation..."

The list goes on and on. From the exotic locale of Nepal to the Great Smokey Mountains of Tennessee, from permanent paid positions to overnight stays, you can find an assignment that suits your personality and meets your criteria. Do you want to see what it is like to run a B & B before you decide to renovate that historic home down the road and become an entrepreneur? You can. Does becoming a caretaker on an estate that is only occupied by its owner two months out of every year appeal to you? Have you fantasized about leaving the city and trying out life in the country? Do you think you'd like running a cat sanctuary for a week while the manager takes a vacation? There is a whole world of remarkable opportunity and adventure awaiting you if you are willing to step out of your comfort zone and try house sitting.

Let's get started by looking at what house sitting is and how it can be very different from caretaking. The two terms are often used interchangeably, but as you'll see in Chapter 2, we think there can be distinct and meaningful differences.

Chapter 2

HOUSE SITTING & CARETAKING — OUR DEFINITIONS

House sitting involves taking care of someone's home (and in many cases pets) with the same care that you would your own. The routine daily chores such as cleaning, taking out the trash, mowing the lawn, doing some weeding, watering plants, bringing in the mail and responding to an unforeseen maintenance issue in an appropriate and timely manner can all be part of the house sitting responsibilities that the homeowner entrusts to you. Special requests may be made. You may be asked to pay bills, or start up their vehicle occasionally so the battery doesn't run down, or answer their business phone line. Each homeowner has their unique needs, but in general, your obligation is to be a presence in the home and maintain it to the standard in which it was presented to you. Many homeowners have pets and they need care and attention. Feeding, walking, bathing, and, in some cases, giving medications or injections may be required. You may receive compensation for your service or you may not. The majority of house sitting positions are unpaid.

While the term "caretaking" is often used synonymously with "house sitting", in reality it generally requires a greater level of commitment on your part   The Caretaker's Gazette, a print and on-line newspaper, advertises caretaking positions that range from the standard house sitting duties mentioned above to full time estate management that pays in excess of $100K a year. Many times caretakers are given a place to live either seasonally or for a longer term in exchange for a specified number of hours of labor. Caretaking positions may include such tasks as:

- grounds maintenance, light construction, handyman services
- housekeeping, cooking, shopping, serving meals, chauffeuring and other types of domestic assistance
- helping on a ranch or farm, maintaining an orchard, taking care of large animals, installing fences or irrigation systems
- managing and maintenance of campgrounds, resorts, bed and breakfasts, hostels
- providing personal assistance, managing staff or events

These are but a few examples of what caretaking can entail. Depending upon the situation, your duties, and what is provided to you in exchange, you may also receive monetary compensation for your services. If this type of position is what you are seeking, we've found no greater resource than the Caretaker's Gazette. Founded in 1983, and dedicated to the caretaking field, they advertise positions available the world over. They can be found at www.caretaker.org. (More on that resource in Chapter 4.)

Which is right for you? Careful self-assessment is the key to answering that question and we'll do that next in Chapter 3.

Chapter 3

DETERMINING YOUR COMFORT ZONE

If you've ever worked in the corporate world, you've probably had experience with assessing the strengths and weaknesses of your company and your competition. If not, it's an insightful experience and one we recommend you perform before venturing into the world of house sitting.

Why do you need to think about your strengths and your limitations? Because knowing them is essential to selecting house sitting positions that you will enjoy and be good at. You also need to think about what you really need in life to be comfortable and what it is you are willing to do without. Your goal should be to provide the best service you can to the homeowner and to do that you must be honest about your own needs and your own boundaries. Picking a location is easy, but picking the right house sit in that location takes some thought.

As an example, we once spent two weeks in discussion with a homeowner regarding the care of their multi-acre property in Hawaii. It was an assignment that would last several months in a great location, the home had gorgeous ocean views and there was one pet to take care of. Sounds ideal, right? But something kept nagging at us and we found it difficult to make the commitment. After talking it through, we realized that the homeowner's expectations for security of their large property and the removal of people who shouldn't be there were beyond our comfortable capabilities. We knew we were capable of it, but we just wouldn't be comfortable doing it. Understanding our own limitations kept us from creating an unhappy situation for ourselves and for the homeowner.

What follows is a brief list of questions to get you started thinking about your own capabilities and what you can honestly, and comfortably, provide to a homeowner.

Self-Assessment 101

1. How strong are you physically? Can you lift a 50 lb. dog or is a Chihuahua more like it? Are you physically able to do what the homeowner needs you to do? Are stairs going to be a problem for you? Can you walk to the store and carry your groceries home if transportation isn't going to be readily available? Be aware of how any physical limitation you may have could possibly prevent you from doing a chore expected by a homeowner.

2. Do you have allergies to pets or other materials that you will come into contact with that will cause ongoing discomfort? How do you feel about bugs? In some places there are a lot of them and they can be large. Spraying may be a common practice. Is that a problem for you?

3. Are you able to function in all types of weather? We once did a house sit in the tropics during summer in 105-degree weather and 60% humidity. It was bearable, but we probably wouldn't do it again! What about an elevation change? Do you get headaches above 10,000 feet? Do you suffer sinus problems in dry climates? Do you get blue if the sun doesn't appear regularly? Do you love cool weather, like the snow?

4. Do you need every modern convenience to be happy? Will you be satisfied without high-speed Internet or television? Do you need a washer and dryer or are you willing to use a Laundromat or a laundry service?

5. How handy are you? Are you able and willing to manage the systems required for maintaining a pool, a well, or living off of the grid? Can you run the lawnmower over that acre of grass or weed that large organic garden?

6. Do you truly love animals? Most homeowners consider their pets to be an important member of the family and have high expectations that you will not only provide for their physical care, but also their emotional well-being. Are you comfortable giving medications or injections to animals if necessary? Have you any experience with older animals?

7. Do you have special dietary requirements that you may not be able to meet in a particular country?

8. Are you willing to use public transportation if you do not have access to a vehicle?

9. Will you be reasonably happy in a country where you do not speak the language? Are you willing to learn a few words so that you can comfortably get along?

10. Lastly, how patient are you? How easily do you become frustrated? How flexible and willing are you to get out of your comfort zone?

There is no right or wrong answer to these questions. They are simply food for thought and, hopefully, will serve to help you filter through the available house sits and find ones that best suit you and meet your needs. A little forethought and self-examination will go a long way helping to identify the ones that won't and minimize your chance of having a negative house sitting experience.

Now that you have a better idea of what you are looking for, just how will you go about finding these wonderful opportunities we keep talking about? In the next chapter we'll give you the best options we've found for locating house sits.

Chapter 4

HOW TO FIND THE PERFECT HOUSE SIT

It will come as no surprise to you that the best place to find house sitting opportunities is on the Internet. What may come as a surprise is that there are only a handful of sites that are viable options for broad geographic searches. There are also regional sites that you can search if you have a specific city in say, Australia, you might want to visit. With the growing interest in house sitting, we would expect that there will be more sites developing for global placement in the near future. Here, we review the best sites with broad geographic reach.

Note: We know that you will want to immediately check out these sites and we encourage you to do that. While you are there, take a look at some of the sitter profiles and homeowner advertisements for house sits. Most of the sites will let you look for free, you just can't apply. It will get you excited! However, preparing your profile and presenting yourself as a great candidate should be a well thought out process so don't rush into doing it. We'll work through the nuts and bolts of creating your profile and marketing yourself in the best way possible in subsequent chapters.

There are commonalities to all of these sites and there are subtle differences too. We'll cover the common items first and then get into some particulars for each site.

In general, all of the sites offer:

- Mechanisms for presenting a profile of yourself along with references and photos. Some sites also have the option of adding a personal video. Some will let you upload your police clearance letters and other types of documents.
- Preference settings for their search engines for such things as the locations in which you are interested, the length of time you desire for a house sit stay and the types of pets you are willing to care for.
- Search options for house sitting assignments. The sites vary from each other in the way that you do this and the ease of accomplishing it.
- Internal messaging systems for contacting homeowners through the site and for having homeowners contact you.
- Privacy options for sharing your information. For instance, you may elect to use the sites internal messaging system in initial communications with a homeowner rather than sharing your personal e-mail address and contact numbers.
- Options for homeowners to review the house sitter profiles and to initiate contact with house sitters.

- No fees for homeowners to list their house sit on the site. This encourages listings.
- Fees for house sitters to fully access and use the site.
- Good marketing of their sites. These sites usually rank highly in an Internet search and come up on the first page or two on the major search engines.

What these sites will not do is match you up with specific homeowners and house sits. They also do not guarantee that you will be chosen to house sit. That is why creating an appealing profile is so important and why we will spend a good amount of time in preparing to market ourselves.

Now let's move on to the site-specific information, including contact information and fees.

Housecarers.com

As with all the sites mentioned here, Housecarers provides a variety of tools to help you create your profile, share your references, load your photos and search listings for house sits. But Housecarers offers a few tools not found on other sites that can be helpful. One is a calendar to keep track of your availability and assignments. You have the option of keeping the calendar private or you can share it with homeowners who are searching the listings for house sitters available on specific dates.

Another useful tool on Housecarers is the means to check stats on the number of visits your profile page is receiving. This can be valuable information if you aren't getting responses to your inquiries for house sits. Maybe you need to change your headline or rewrite some of your personal copy?

Housecarers also allows you to display your direct contact information if you choose, speeding up the process for the homeowner to contact you directly rather than going through the sites internal message system. (Your e-mail is encrypted to reduce spam.)

There is a large amount of space allowed on Housecarers for your photos and references, up to 14 of each and you can link your website, blog and Facebook page to your profile. The additional photos, references and site links help the homeowner get a better picture of who you are and will perhaps interest them enough to interview you. You also receive a personal URL that links to your profile page. Your URL can then be used on business cards and other marketing materials directing people to look at your profile page.

Housecarers proactively e-mails new sitter listings to homeowners who have requested this service, bringing you to their attention. This can be very useful as some homeowners choose not to advertise their own house sits but to search out house sitters and contact them. They will also notify you by e-mail as new listing become available in areas that you select.

Housecarers support material includes a sample house sitting agreement. Whether you use a formal written agreement or not, reading the samples on the various sites is a good idea. They provide insight into the types of things you may need to discuss with a homeowner before you begin your house sitting experience.

The annual fee for joining Housecarers is $50 per year as of this writing. Housecarers does offer a free trial membership but you will not be able to apply for house sits until you upgrade to the full membership.

Lastly, Housecarers offers an affiliate program so you earn a commission on referrals to their site if you so choose.

MindMyHouse.com

One of the things that we like about MindMyHouse is the variety of options they give the user for performing searches. Their use of keywords in the search options area allows you to customize your search for an assignment not only by location, but by other criteria as well. This can help you fine tune your house sit search and spend less time looking at ads that are not of interest.

Another useful option MindMyHouse offers is the ability to search in order of the latest listings first to see what has just come up in a given area. This is helpful, because the sooner you apply for a house sit after its initial listing, the more chance you have of the homeowner taking a good look at you as a possibility. Popular assignments can generate so many responses for an owner that they may not look at all of the submissions. It may be a cliché, but when it comes to house sitting, the early bird very often does get the worm!

Although we recommend that you do your own daily search on the sites that you join when you are in house-hunting mode, MindMyHouse will send you notifications of house sitting ads as they are posted. Receiving these e-mails can bring attention to house sitting assignments in particular locations or timeframes that you may have overlooked or not considered. You can select to receive these notifications daily, weekly, or not at all.

MindMyHouse also offers the use of "short-lists" so when you do a search and see an ad that interests you, you can add it to a short-list. You can make notes on your shortlist for each ad and can contact the homeowner via e-mail directly from that page. It is a handy way of keeping track of the ads you come across particularly when you are doing a large search.

MindMyHouse presents the homeowner with house sitter ads based on the criteria set by the homeowner for their search. However, the ads that meet the criteria are presented in random order rather than by how long you have belonged to the site or some other ranking system. What this means to you, as a new house sitter, is that you have as much chance to come up first in a search as house sitters with experience! When you are starting out this is certainly a valuable consideration.

MindMyHouse's support materials include a sample house sitting agreement and before-you-go checklists for homeowners and house sitters. They have a member blog, a Facebook page, and mobile compatibility making it easy to check the site from your mobile device.

At MindMyHouse your profile page is given its own URL that you can use on business cards and marketing materials and as a link to your personal website or blog.

The fee to join MindMyHouse is $20 per year as of this writing.

TrustedHouseSitters.com

TrustedHousesitters.com operates a little differently than the two sites we've already discussed. While the mechanics of presenting a profile, searching for house sits and being searched out by homeowners are similar, TrustedHousesitters.com maintains a tighter control on the information that is being presented. For instance, once your profile has been reviewed and "accepted", you will want to add references to the site. In order to do this, you must apply through TrustedHousesitters.com who will then e-mail the source of your reference. They do this in order to prevent anyone from providing altered or false references. While at first glance this may seem cumbersome, it does add an extra measure of confidence for the homeowner that you are credible. As with any other relationship in life, trust is the key, and TrustedHousesitters.com is focused on building that for their clientele.

Another feature that is different from other sites is their ranking system. TrustedHousesitters.com scores house sitters by a variety of factors including number of references you've provided, number of photos you've posted, and if you've uploaded a video of yourself. They also give you points for having a police clearance letter, but they don't allow you to post the letter on the site for security reasons. The points you are awarded determine how high you sit on the search positioning. While this may seem to create an uneven playing field, keep in mind that references can be from past or present employers, landlords and/or personal character references. As someone without house sitting experience, we recommend that you collect these types of references anyway to post on whatever site(s) that you join. A homeowner may not be concerned with your actual house sitting experience if they believe that you are trustworthy, responsible and will do a good job for them. Everyone has to start somewhere!

The fee structure for TrustedHousesitters.com is also unlike the other sites in that they encourage a homeowner to look for a house sitter and post an ad, but then the homeowner must pay a fee to make contact with the potential house sitter. At this writing, homeowner's fees range from $15.00 for one month of access to $60.00 for one year. Additionally, their fee structure for house sitters works slightly different in that they offer 3, 6, and 12-month memberships for $30.00, $45.00 and $60.00 respectively.

HousesittersAmerica.com

House Sitters America is just what it sounds like. It is strictly focused on posting house sitting opportunities for the United States. While not as large or as versatile in the offering of tools as other sites, it does provide focused access to potential house sits across America.

House Sitters America also has an interesting system for how it determines the order in which house sitters come up in a homeowner's search. Their list is ordered by the most recent house sitters to log into their site. The thinking being active house sitters who are searching will be using the site frequently, while those house sitters who aren't active won't be looking for assignments. This then allows the "active house sitters to float to the top" of a homeowners search. Our advice, once again, is to visit your sites daily when you are looking for a house sit.

The cost to join House Sitters America is $30.00 per year.

Caretaker.Org

Caretaker.org is the website for the Caretaker's Gazette, on on-line and print publication that has been advertising caretaking assignments since 1983. Its stated claim to fame is that it is the only publication in the world dedicated to the caretaking field. As the name implies, its focus is on caretaking positions. As we discussed in Chapter 2, caretaking can vary from what we would consider to be house sitting to full time salaried positions with benefits. While we have found that the majority of the ads listed in the Caretaker's Gazette fall into the caretaking category as we define it, they do have some ads for what we would consider as house sitting. Their scope is broad – in the latest issue published at this writing, there were more than 100 caretaking opportunities in 33 states and 20 countries. If caretaking is what you are looking for, this is an invaluable publication. If not, well, the variety of offerings are fascinating reading to say the least!

The Caretaker's Gazette is published monthly and, at this writing, cost $29.95 per year for an on-line subscription and $34.95 for a print subscription.

You may, at this point, be trying to figure out if there is a "best" site among those that we have discussed here. Truthfully, they all have their strengths and weaknesses when it comes to how the sites function. But the important point is that they all work. They get the job done and they do help you to find house sitting positions that are available around the world. We use, and belong to, all of them. While you may be thinking that you don't want to make that kind of investment initially, you could think of it in terms of the money that you will eventually save by house sitting as compared to the cost of a vacation. If you are feeling uncertain take a look at them and pick one just to get started. The important thing is to start!

We've covered quite a bit of material here, and if you are feeling slightly overwhelmed by it all, don't. Once you've spent some time looking at these sites, it all begins to fall into place.

Be proactive in creating your own opportunities

While Internet sites are the way to gain access to a wide range of house sitting opportunities there are some other things that you can do to market yourself. Here are a few of the strategies that we've come across:

- Create a business card (with a link to your profile page on the site that you've joined, and your personal website or blog) and hand it out whenever you have the opportunity. Don't be shy about it. You never know who is going to need a house sitter or know someone who's going to.
- Post your card and/or flyer on bulletin boards at locations that you frequent. If the coffee shop where you buy your latte every morning or your local library has a community bulletin board, use it. Do some local sits — even for just a weekend — it can be a great way to gain some experience and build up your reference letter collection.
- Offer your services to friends, family members or co-workers for a weekend to gain experience. Just make sure they understand that you expect a nice reference letter for the good job that you've done!
- Talk about what you are planning to do. Spread the word to anyone and everyone. Again, you never know who has a cabin in the mountains that they would rather not leave empty in the off-season.

If you are uncomfortable with the idea of promoting yourself, please keep in mind that house sitting is a mutually beneficial relationship. Both homeowner and house sitter benefit. Not only are you offering a valuable service, but if you do a good job, you will have given the homeowner a great gift — a worry free vacation from the routine of their normal lives. So talk it up, share what you do, build up a network. We've found that most people are quite interested in hearing about our adventures and curious about how house sitting works.

Next, in Chapter 5, we're going to work through the process of creating the professional profile that you need to become a successful house sitter.

Chapter 5

CREATING A PROFILE THAT GETS RESULTS

If you haven't already spent some time perusing the web sites that we discussed in the previous chapter, now would be a good time to do it. Look at the house sitter profiles. These folks are the competition. Yes, we know that sounds a bit too much like business and not like the fun thing we expect house sitting to be. But, it's true because there are more house sitters than there are house sitting assignments. We recently looked at the numbers on one of the house sitting sites and found 12 house sitters registered for every house sit advertised. That is not to say that all were active and searching at the same time, but you will have competition for a good sit. So what do you do? You make yourself look as good as you possibly can to the homeowner who will be searching through those profiles and that's what we are going to do here. (You also pro-actively search for house sits but we'll cover that in Chapter 7.)

For simplicity we'll create your profile in the same order in which the sites have you enter the information so you can copy and paste it directly from your word-processing document.

Profile Titles

The first thing that you will be asked for is your profile title. What are the words that come to mind that describe you and what you have to offer? Keep in mind that the titles not only need to say something about you, but they need to say something about you that the homeowner will want! Simply saying that you are a "40 something writer seeking an assignment in Bali" doesn't really say much about what you have to offer a homeowner. So, think about your situation and what characteristics, skills and knowledge you have to offer a homeowner. Are you:

- Retired – if you are, this is great because it indicates that you have years of life experience to draw upon. You've probably had a responsible job, maintained a house, a garden, have some "DIY skills", cared for pets. Also, if you have reached this stage in life, you can appreciate the effort it takes to obtain and maintain a house. You understand how much of an investment it is for the homeowner. Using the word "retired" in your title can work in your favor because it implies maturity. We suggest though, if you use it, you should combine it with words that imply you are still energetic enough to do the job. Words like "lively", "active", "youthful", "physically fit", "robust", "hearty" "vital", "energetic", "enthusiastic", and "dynamic" bring across that message and work well when used with words such as "mature", "experienced" and "retired".

- Employed – Are you "professional", "responsible", "reliable", "capable", and "knowledgeable"? Is there something you do in your professional life that can be applied to house sitting? Does your job require you to be "meticulous", "hands-on", and "skillful"? Are you "expert", "qualified", "experienced", "established" or "trained"? You must be some or all of these or you wouldn't be employed! As with any interview, you must use words that build upon your strengths and convince a homeowner you are the best candidate for the "job".

- Changing lifestyles or in an evolving situation – are you a teacher on sabbatical, a grad student working on a thesis, in between careers, thinking about chucking it all and moving out of the country, uncertain about the next steps in your life? Perhaps you are "well-organized", "fastidious", "flexible", "dependable", "dedicated", a "homebody", "conscientious", "well-educated", or "a white glove house keeper" who loves to clean? Do you have a "green thumb" or a "can do attitude"? Are you a "confident" caretaker? Whatever your situation may be at the moment, find positive words that best describe what you have to offer the homeowner.

- Young in age— do you have "energy" in abundance? Are you "enthusiastic" or "excited"? Do you bring a youthful "exuberance" to your assignments? Are you "passionate" about animals, "devoted" to their care and well-being? Are you "strong" or "hard-working" and willing to do some manual labor? Are you "sincere", "trustworthy", "and "respectful"? You may not have had that many life or job experiences to draw upon yet, but if you are considering house sitting then you are certainly "creative", and "resourceful" and "adaptable". Your task will be to convince the homeowner that you are "mature" and "responsible" enough to handle the assignment.

By now you've realized that these categories are simply a way of presenting and organizing the considerable number of ways you could describe yourself in a positive and meaningful way. Any of the words could possibly be the perfect words to describe what you have to offer as a house sitter. The important thing is to write a title that actively portrays your attributes. So, take all of the words that describe you, make a list, and set it aside. We're not going to write your title just yet because we need to work on your introduction first and the two go hand in hand.

Profile Introduction

Next to the title, this is the most important section of your profile. This is where you will write a brief introduction of yourself. Note the word brief. The key here is to provide enough description that the homeowner will get a sense of who you are, but not be overwhelmed. This isn't the place for your life story. In addition to providing a short introduction of yourself, you should also use this area to make some statements about what you have to offer the homeowner. Why do this in the intro area? Because when a homeowner does a search for a house sitter, a list is generated providing a small picture, the title and the first two or three lines of text from the introduction section. So, in effect, these first few lines are really an extension of your headline and will be the first thing the homeowner sees about you. They create the homeowner's first impression of you. You must grab the homeowner's attention at this point so they open up your main profile page. If you don't capture them now, they may continue to browse through the ads and never return to actually see your full profile. So how do you hone in on the key information you want to present in these first few lines? We're going to take the list we started with our "attribute words" and add statements that introduce us and describe any experience we have that may interest the homeowner. We recommend doing this in a list format initially because it forces you to be concise & focused. Here are three examples:

retired, widow, age 63	professional couple, mid-40's	24-year-old student, single
financial advisor	realtor & teacher	majoring in biology
own historic home	own home & rental unit	live at home with parents
speak three languages	former peace-corps volunteers	organic gardener
world traveler	teach English as 2nd language	vegan
volunteer teaching English	show horses, equestrians	spent summer in Europe
play chess, read, write	experience with landscaping	play soccer & like hiking
remodeled own home	love cats & dogs	have construction experience
raised on a farm	extensive travel experience	like hands on work, am strong
physically fit, exercise	do yoga & meditate	had hamsters & guinea pigs
home-body, gourmet cook	keep immaculate house	like to be organized

Now take your list of words that you developed for the title and add them to this list. For example:

63 year old widow	40's professional couple	student
energetic	reliable	responsible
mature	trustworthy	honest
experienced	flexible, easy going	hard-working
physically fit	committed	respectful
qualified	expert	skilled
knowledgeable	conscientious	caring

Next, take a minute and put a check next to the words that you think will make the best impression on the homeowner. Then, write a title and an introductory paragraph that includes your chosen words and is no more than 4-5 lines long including at least one statement that indicates what you can do for the homeowner.

We recommend that all of the writing for your profile be created in short paragraphs. It appears more appealing to the reader than a long, run-on, block of text and is much more likely to be read through.

Here are some samples of headline text and first introductory paragraphs for our example house sitters:

<u>Energetic, Retired Home Body, Specializes in Caring for Historic Homes and B & B's</u>

I'm 63, physically fit, organized and dedicated to providing careful attention to your home or B & B. I've remodeled a historic home and can handle any maintenance issues that might arise. As a gourmet cook, I'm expert at preparing breakfasts at your B & B while you take a vacation!

Equestrian Couple Will Provide Expert Care of Your Home & Horses

We're a professional couple in our 40's with all the skills and experience needed to care for your home and equine family. We're committed to providing the best care for them and for your home. We're experienced homeowners and landlords so we understand the value of your home and possessions.

Grad Student and Skilled Organic Gardener Willing to Work Hard Taking Care of Your Home & Yard

I'm a responsible 24-year old student, with a green thumb, who loves working hard and working outside. I'm honest and reliable, and need a quiet place to work on my thesis in exchange for taking care of your home, garden, and/or doing some light construction or landscaping work.

As you can see, with very few words we managed to accomplish several key things:

- We've briefly described ourselves (age, status, situation)

- We've provided some information about our special skills and what we can offer a homeowner
- We've given some indication as to our character and our values ("dedicated", "committed", "honest")

All of this information was presented in a positive way. We did not say that "we have no experience but..." We all have experiences to draw upon that can be directly related to house sitting and that is what you want to emphasize. At this point, elaborate further in a few short paragraphs. But remember, no negative statements and keep the tone upbeat.

What we have to offer as house sitters

This is generally the next category that the sites will want you to complete. This is an elaboration on what you have briefly stated above. In this area you can provide more detail, such as the number of years that you have cared for pets, the specific types of pets, the types of project you've worked on that gave you the experience you've stated you have, your language or volunteer skills that may be applicable, etc. Again, use short paragraphs, concise language, and a positive tone.

Why I want to house sit?

This is another common profile question. As we've mentioned before, we consider house sitting to be a mutually beneficial arrangement, so don't be uncomfortable in sharing your own hoped for house sitting outcomes. The homeowner will appreciate knowing your motivations. It will help them understand if you are a good match for their home and location. Frequently people want to house sit because:

- They love to travel and want to broaden their horizons, meet new people and experience other cultures
- They are learning a new language and want to have the opportunity to practice it daily with native speakers
- They are looking for a place that provides solitude so they can focus on some project — often writing or school work
- They love animals and enjoy taking care of them
- They want to experience a different lifestyle — city to country, homeowner to apartment dweller, on the grid to off the grid, etc.
- They want a change in weather — from home where it's below zero all winter to the tropics or vice-versa

- They want to learn about something that is available in the homeowner's area — regional cooking, types of music, traditional folk or fine art created in that locale, etc.

These are but a few of the many reasons people give for house sitting. You may have your own unique reasons. Whatever they are, be honest with the homeowner as to why it is you think house sitting is going to be a desirable situation for yourself. The homeowner wants you to be happy and satisfied so that you will enjoy taking good care of their home.

Whatever your situation, please remember to put a good face on it if you are doing it as a result of a life event that is less than positive. If you are having financial difficulties that preclude you from traveling, you don't need to say that. You can simply state that house sitting makes travel more affordable to you. If you are in a life transition and uncertain of what your next steps are, you can say that you "want to experience another lifestyle" or "broaden your horizons". You get the idea. A homeowner wants to leave you in charge of their home knowing that you are capable and happy to be there. The last thing they want when they go away is to worry about their house sitter.

Photos

We cannot over emphasize the importance of putting your photograph on your profile page. The homeowner wants to see the person they are considering interviewing. This photo should feature you fairly close up, at least close enough to see you clearly, smiling, and looking happy. We are always surprised when we see photos of house sitters looking glum or actually frowning. Why would anyone want to get to know someone who looks like they are in a bad mood? You want to create a welcoming visual presence, inviting the homeowner to get to know you.

Instructions for uploading photos are given on every site and are easy to follow. Some sites allow for more than one photo. We encourage you to post as many as you can. Pack these photos full of visual information which underscores the written information you've presented about yourself in the profile section. This is the perfect place for that photo of you on your kite board (an example of your adventurous nature), or working in the garden (let them see how hard you work), or walking the dog. Use this area to your full advantage to visually market yourself.

Other profile information

This is where you will include information such as references, police clearance letters and criminal background checks, certifications, websites, blogs or other social media contact information.

We're going to tackle putting all these pieces together in the next chapter. In the meantime, your task is to draft your completed profile in your word processor and run the spelling and grammar check. When you are finished, please pat yourself on the back. You've just completed a big step in the preparation process.

After you've read through the next chapter, and have gathered your references and other materials together, you can paste your profile into the site(s) you've chosen and upload the rest. Just follow the directions given on that particular site.

Once you've completed these steps you are good to go! You are now a house sitter on the search for your first assignment.

Chapter 6

PROFILE EXTRAS – THE EFFORT IS WORTH IT

In this category falls all of the extra information that you provide a homeowner in addition to your profile. Most of the websites we've discussed will let you upload some, or all, of these documents for easy access by the homeowner. Alternatively, you can keep these documents private, and share them with a homeowner after you have begun communication.

We'll start with references and then move on to police clearance letters, criminal background checks, driver's licenses and international driver's permits.

References – how do you obtain them without experience?

Even if you've never done any house sitting you still have plenty of resources for obtaining reference letters. You just need to be a little creative and resourceful. We had three good letters to provide to homeowners when we began house sitting. Two were character references, one from a friend and one from a business associate. The third letter was from a woman from whom we had rented a vacation home. That was all we had and it was enough to get us started.

Reference letter contents

The basic information your reference letters should provide is a description of the relationship the writer has to you (landlord, friend, business associate, etc.), a statement describing how their relationship to you qualifies them to give a reference (they've rented to you, entrusted the care of their pets to you, employed you, known you for 15 years, etc.), and the reasons why they recommend you (you're trustworthy, you follow through with your commitments, your work ethic is exemplary, your care of their property was outstanding, etc.). Each letter needs the reference providers home or business address, phone contact numbers and e-mail address. You want to make it as convenient as possible for the homeowner to reach them for verification. We've found that some homeowners contacted our references for verification and some felt that doing a personal or Skype interview gave them the assurance they needed to be confident in selecting us. You need to be prepared for either circumstance.

Think about whom you know that would be a good reference for you. Someone you trust to be excited about this new step you are taking in your life. You want that kind of enthusiasm to come through when they are called upon personally to speak with a homeowner. You also want to pick someone you know will be reliable in responding in a timely manner to a homeowner's inquiry.

<u>Personal references</u>

We recommend personal references from people that you have known for more than a short time. We think it gives more weight to their opinion if they can state that they have known you for a number of years. Do you have friends that you have stayed with or vacationed with? Do you have former or current roommates that you are on good terms with? Can they speak to your neatness, your house keeping abilities, your financial responsibility? Maybe they have been visitors to your home numerous times and can attest to how well you keep it, how handy you are, or how much effort you put into maintaining your yard or garden. Perhaps you've done some volunteer work with this person and they can verify that you were committed and reliable. Pick people who have known you for a while and can speak with knowledge about your character, your reliability, your resourcefulness, and your trustworthiness.

Business references

When we began house sitting we had already been retired for a few years so our business relationships had either faded away or morphed into friendships. If that is the case for you, don't fret. You still do business in life. You have an attorney, a banker, an accountant or a financial planner. There is the president of your condo association, your women's club chairperson, and the executive director of the non-profit where you do your volunteer work every week. Think of all the people with whom you have on-going relationships that are not personal friends. These are people who know you in a different context than your friends. They too can speak to your honesty, reliability, sense of responsibility, and your capabilities.

If you are still working, you will have many choices from your current and former work colleagues. Zero in on the best of them. Who has had the most direct contact with you? Who would have first-hand knowledge of your talents, your professionalism, your organizational skills, and your willingness to go that extra mile in a pinch? Your boss believed in you enough to hire you so maybe he or she would be willing to be your reference.

Resources from vacation rentals, landlords and tenants

If you are a renter, or a former renter, you can contact the landlord or management company and ask for a reference. Who better to speak about your treatment of a property than someone who has rented to you? If you have ever rented a vacation property for a period of time, perhaps the property owner would help you out by providing a reference. Another source for a letter that is often overlooked is your own tenants if you have rental property. They can certainly verify that you respond to maintenance issues in a timely manner, that you delivered the house to them in spotless condition, that the landscaping has been well maintained, that you've been forthright in your dealings and followed through on your promises.

Having trouble getting references?

If you are finding that the people you contact are hesitant to provide a reference, find out why. If you have some unresolved issue, perhaps this is a good time to deal with it and get it out of the way. Sometimes though, people are simply uncomfortable with their own ability to express themselves or feel their writing skills are not up to par. They may or may not tell you this.

But, if you sense some hesitancy, and you know you have a great relationship and there is no good reason for them not to do this for you, that may be what is hindering them. At this point, we suggest that you offer to provide a draft of a letter that they can work from, adding their own personal touches. Here is a sample of one such letter:

To Whom It May Concern:

I have known _____ for ____ years in a personal (or professional) capacity. As a volunteer (or co-worker) with the ABC organization I worked with _____ on many projects. I experienced first-hand her excellent communication skills, friendliness, respect and concern for others, and her high level of dedication to meeting the commitments she makes.

I've also had the opportunity to visit _____ 's home and observed that she takes great care and pride in maintaining it to a high standard. I know that she did some remodeling work (or gardening, landscaping, painting, etc.) to the home and her do-it-yourself abilities are impressive. I would entrust the care of my home to _____ without hesitation.

In my opinion, _____ is highly qualified to house sit and I give her my most sincere recommendation. If I can provide any further information, please feel free to contact me.

Sincerely,

Name, Address, phone number and e-mail address

You could also include a statement pertaining to pet care such as:

"_____ has had a variety of pets including dogs, cats, and parakeets during the time that I've known her and I've seen the love and care that she has given them. She is truly a pet person! She makes very effort to give her pets the best quality of life."

Hopefully, providing such a sample letter will do the trick!

If someone is hesitant because they are uncertain about making the time for returning an e-mail or a phone call inquiry, then perhaps asking them to be a reference only until you have completed your first assignment will work for them. At that point, you can replace their letter with the glowing letter of endorsement you received from the homeowner!

If, in the end, you find their resistance to be unwavering thank the person politely for considering it and move on. You don't want to force the issue because even if they gave you the reference letter they probably will not willingly or enthusiastically respond to homeowners e-mail or phone call inquiry anyway.

Police clearance letters & criminal background checks

Providing a police clearance letter or a copy of a criminal background check provides the homeowner with another layer of assurance that you are who you say you are and you have no criminal history. Some house sitters have them, but certainly not all. Is it necessary? To the homeowners who places little importance on this type of document, no. To a homeowner who needs every assurance possible in order to feel truly comfortable having you in their home, with their possessions, it is. Did we obtain them? Yes. Do we use it? Yes, we do, but not all of the time. We offer the option to the homeowner and let them decide if they want to see it. We recommend that you obtain one because as a newcomer to the house sitting world you have not built up a library of references from satisfied homeowners. This document is an additional way to create confidence in the homeowner that you are the candidate they should select. There are a variety of options for obtaining these documents depending upon if you want a local, statewide, or national search. The more extensive the search, the costlier they are.

We obtained local police clearance letters which covered a geographic area pertinent to where we were residing. These can usually be obtained directly from your local police department. There will be a fee, and usually they will take your fingerprints. We paid $30.00 (U.S.) per person and it took about 3 days to receive them. If this option interests you we recommend that you contact your local police department and begin with them. If they don't provide this service they will certainly know where to direct you.

For background checks that cover a broader geographic area do a Google search. Where we were living the State Attorney General's office processes statewide background checks. They too require fingerprints. Some places still take paper prints but most require live scan prints. There is usually a FAQ area on the website that explains the process and the cost. For example, the fee in our State (not including the fingerprinting) is $25.00 (U.S.) and the process takes up to 2 weeks to complete.

National background checks are done by the FBI in the U.S., by the Royal Canadian Mounted Police in Canada, through the Criminal Records Bureau in the U.K., and in Australia by the Australian Federal Police. Here are the websites:

U.S.	www.fbi.gov/about-us/cjis/background-checks
Canada	www.rcmp-grc.cg.ca
U.K.	www.disclosure.gov.uk
Australia	www.afp.gov.au

You may be asked by a homeowner to provide a copy of your driver's license or passport for identification. This is simply a way for the homeowner to be certain that you are indeed who you claim to be. Homeowners who use house sitters tend to be trusting by nature but in today's world security is important.

A homeowner may offer you the use of their vehicle. If they do they may want to see a copy of your driver's license. If they do offer you the use of their vehicle you need to determine if you will be covered under their auto insurance policy or your own in the event of an accident.

International Driver's Permits

In addition to our State issued driver's license, we also obtained International Driving Permits (IDP). These are useful if you will be traveling out of your own country. It is a passport size document with translations in several foreign languages and can be used as valid identification in 174 countries. You must travel with your country of origin's license along with the IDP. In the U.S., the State Department has approved two sources for the IDP. They are the American Automobile Association (www.aaa.com) and the National Auto Club (www.thenac.com). In Canada an IDP can be obtained from the Canadian Automobile Association (www.CAA.ca/travel/travel-permits-e.cfm). A completed application form, two passport sized photos, a copy of your driver's license (which must be valid for at least 6 months past the date of your IDP issuance) are required. At this writing, they cost $15.00 in the U.S. and $25.00 in Canada. They are valid for one year and can be obtained via mail. For more information and applications see the websites.

Certifications, Licenses, Special Training

You may have had some special training in an area that is applicable to your house sitting role. If so, we recommend that you include the information. Once again, anything that is going to give you, the new kid on the block, an edge is worth publicizing.

<u>Websites, Blogs, Social Media</u>

If you participate in Facebook or another social media platform, have your own website or blog, it's a good idea to link it to your profile page if the house sitting site makes this available to you. Again, you will be expanding the homeowner's ability to get to know you and increasing your chances of getting the assignment. But before you do, take a good look at all of your postings through the eyes of a homeowner looking for a house sitter. If there is anything that doesn't seem appropriate either remove it or opt to skip the link.

Another option we recommend is linking your house sitting site URL, which links directly to your personal profile page, to your social media site, website or blog. This announces your new venture and may generate some house sitting opportunities.

<u>A closing thought about the "extras"</u>

If the house sitting site you use does not allow for uploading information beyond standard references you will want to state in your profile that you have these items available upon request drawing the homeowner's attention to their existence. We do this and then e-mail the documents in PDF format to the homeowner when asked.

Chapter 7

GETTING THE ASSIGNMENT THAT YOU WANT

Okay, you've put your profile up, your references are in order, and the photos you've posted look great. Now, how do you find and get the house sit that you desire? Well, we'll get to that in just a moment. Before we do, we recommend that if you are applying for a house sitting assignment in an area unfamiliar to you that you do some important research first. This is what we suggest:

- If you are going out of your country of residence find out if a visa is required in addition to your passport and what the visa requirements and restrictions are. You can find this by doing a Google search. For example, simply type in "visa requirements for Ireland" and you will find it. If you are considering a long- term house sit, determine how long you can legally stay in that country. All countries have limitations.

- If you are going to a location where there may be health concerns such as malaria, you should also check the Center for Disease Control's website (www.cdc.gov/), or your country's equivalent, for updated information on what preventative measures are recommended.

- If you have any doubts about the safety of the particular area, check the U.S. State Department website (www.state.gov/travel/), or your country's equivalent, for travel warnings and recommendations.

- If you are unfamiliar with the location's weather patterns go to a site such as www.weather.com to check the average temperatures for the time of year that you will be visiting.

- A wealth of additional helpful information can be found at Chamber of Commerce sites and visitor Information sites specific to location. Wikipedia, Google and Google Earth are great resources for photographs and information.

Now, let's get back to our search. In Chapter 4 we discussed the various sites and their search options. You have the opportunity to receive alerts from these sites whenever a new house sit posting comes up in the area(s) in which you have indicated your interest and we recommend that you do so. These alerts are great. But the best way to find the house sit you want is to be proactive. You need to check the sites every single day. We do when we are looking for our next assignment. We've found that if we wait for the posting to come through the alert it may have already been posted on the site for a while because some sites only send alerts once a day. A good house sit, in a fantastic location, during a time of year with decent weather, is going to have a lot of respondents. You want to be in the top tier. If you aren't, and there are many applicants, the chances are that the homeowner may not look at all of the responses and you won't even have a chance at it. Having said that, if you do see a particular ad that you are interested in, and it has been posted for a while, you should still apply. Here are a few reasons why:

- Not all house sitting assignments are easy for the homeowner to fill. There are many situations advertised you might find desirable which other house sitters would not. For instance, house sits in remote locations or locations which are expensive and time consuming to travel to. Not everyone wants to drive a quad 15 miles over a dirt road to get their groceries. Not everyone is going to be interested in really labor-intensive sits. Not everyone can handle large animals. Many house sits come up from "snow birds", those folks that want to leave their cold climates for warmer weather. Maybe you really like snowshoeing or cross-country skiing. A lot of house sitters wouldn't even consider it.

- The house sitter that was in the running may have bailed out and that is why the posting is still up.

- Many house sit listings are advertised with "variable" time frames. These folks may not have firm dates yet but they know they are going to need a house sitter and want to line up their options.

- For whatever reason the advertisement didn't get a lot of responses. Maybe it was bad timing — not many people searching for sits. You truly cannot assume anything.

- Because applying takes little time, and even if the assignment is already filled, perhaps the homeowner will keep you in mind for something in the future.

Once you've determined that the house sit fits your desired location, date availability and skill set, you will need to contact the homeowner through the site's internal messaging system. This affords both the homeowner and the house sitter privacy by not revealing your direct contact details.

The letter you write should serve as an introduction, indicate why you are interested in that specific house sit, and have a bit of information about why you would be a good fit for the position. Keep in mind that your objective is to let the homeowner know what you have to offer them. There will be time later to discuss what the position offers you, if you get interviewed. It should be brief, written in short paragraphs, and basically be a mini version of your profile that you have now tailored to the specific assignment. Your full profile will automatically be attached to the letter so they will have that document to flesh out the details. We usually reiterate in our closing that we have references, our police clearance letters, etc., available for their review. You may also, at this point, add that you are willing to provide a security deposit if necessary. Not that many homeowners will ask you for one, but some will, and if you are truly interested in that particular assignment it might be worth considering.

After you've sent the letter, you wait. But you also continue to search the listings for other options and you keep applying for any that interest you.

> Note: We've created a contact log for you at the end of the book to track your house sitting applications and basic data. Make copies for your own use. It's helpful to have on hand.

While it may take only a few hours to hear from a homeowner, it might take a week. Usually, it is within a few days. If the homeowner is interested they will send you an e-mail with additional information and some questions or they will ask for your direct contact information so they can e-mail you directly and/or contact you by phone. If you don't hear anything within a week we recommend sending a follow-up message to them. In this message you should state that you applied for the house sit and still hope to be considered. You should also state something to the effect that you would appreciate being considered for something in the future if this assignment is already filled.

Another situation which may occur is contact initiated by the homeowner. Homeowners will not always post their house sits on a site preferring to search the house sitter listing themselves. If a homeowner is interested in you they will send an e-mail through the sites internal messaging system (or directly to you, if that information is available). Your response letter will be similar to the one we've just discussed but tailored to answer any specific questions that the homeowner may have posed.

Before proceeding, we'd like to make mention of that old-fashioned thing called etiquette. You may be frustrated by a homeowner's lack of timeliness in responding, but you can't let it show, nor can you afford to take your time responding if you are truly interested in the house sit. Your professionalism is what counts. Be polite and responsive at all times in your communications with homeowners. You may not get this assignment but you may very well get a call the next time they need a house sitter.

Interviewing with the Homeowner

Several options can occur once the homeowner has indicated they are interested in you as a potential match for their house sit. Communication may proceed through a series of e-mails, or may jump directly to a phone, Skype, or an in-person interview if it's geographically feasible. If you cannot do an in-person interview we strongly suggest that you Skype. "Meeting" the homeowner creates a sense of confidence and comfort for each of you that written communication cannot.

We like to approach the interview process prepared. It can be a bit awkward in the first minute or two of a Skype video call or a phone call with a stranger and you don't want to give the impression that you are disorganized or uncertain. We suggest a bit of small talk to establish rapport and then letting the homeowner take the lead. Once they have given you their description of what is needed you can proceed to asking your questions.

At this point in your communication we recommend that you ask only the questions you need answered in order to determine if this house sit will work for you. It's entirely possible to overwhelm a homeowner by getting into too many nitty-gritty details too soon. That can wait until you are the one selected! One of our first opportunities to house sit was for a homeowner on the French Riviera. Amateurs that we were, in our excitement we completely overwhelmed the homeowner with questions that were unnecessary at that point. The homeowner's likely impression of us was that we were high-maintenance and fussy. Needless to say, we lost out on a house sit we really wanted.

Take a look at the following list of questions and consider their importance to you in an initial interview. Some of these may be very important, others you may not find of consequence. The most important questions, the deal-breakers so to speak, are what you need to ask.

Keep in mind that these are generalities and you will need to tailor your questions to the specific situation and your requirements. The homeowner's ad may have already answered many of these questions but some homeowners provide very little information in their listings so you should be prepared.

- Ask for a description of what the homeowner expects you to do for them in their absence. Will you basically be a "presence" in the home for security purposes or will you have other responsibilities? If the list of tasks is lengthy, or you are expected to participate in a project, ask how many hours of labor a day or week will be involved.

- If pet care is required this is usually stated in the ad. You should ask how old the pets are and about their care. Do the dogs need daily walking? Do any of the pets require medications or special care?

- Ask the homeowner if they can give you some idea of the accommodations you will have. Generally, the homeowner will give you specifics telling you that you will have access to the whole house, a guesthouse, a private room and bath, etc. If your access is limited to a part of the home you may want to ask if you have the use of the kitchen and laundry.

Ask if they can e-mail you a picture or two of the house and yard.

- We've previously recommended that you check the weather for that location and time period if you are unfamiliar with the area. If you haven't, ask what the weather is like at that time of the year.

- If you are going to be in a tropical climate, and staying cool is important to you, ask if there is air conditioning anywhere in the house. If air conditioning isn't available you may want to ask if the house has fans and screens. Some places have mosquitos or other bugs at certain times of the year and screens may make the difference between a great house sit and a miserable one.

- If the ad indicated you will be responsible for paying utilities ask what they are and for an estimate of the costs involved.

- If the homeowner did not provide any information in their ad regarding the proximity of the home to shopping resources, and you will not have a car, you should ask about transportation options. If you are taking care of pets, and you will not have your own transportation, ask if you will have access to a vehicle to transport the pet(s) to a veterinarian in the event of an emergency.

- If you need Internet access ask if it is available. If not, is there somewhere nearby with Wi-Fi?
- Ask if there is anything else you need to know that hasn't been covered.
- Ask if there is any other information that you can provide for the homeowner.

These are the types of questions that paint a broad picture of what your house sitting assignment will entail. This knowledge, along with the research that you did prior to your applying, should give you enough information to determine if the house sit it appropriate for you.

We recommend that as you proceed through the interview process that you make some positive statements such as "I've got experience with that", "that won't be a problem for me", "I really enjoy doing that", or "I've always wanted to visit your city". If there is something that you don't have experience with, and the homeowner asks you about it, express your willingness to learn. Your enthusiasm needs to be evident and give every indication to the homeowner that you are a good match for their house sitting requirements.

In closing the interview confirm dates for the assignment and ask what the next steps are. End the conversation by thanking them for their consideration and indicate that you think you can do a great job and would enjoy house sitting for them (if this is the case).

We've had owners offer us the position at this point so you must be prepared, based on the answers to your questions, to provide a response. If you want it, it's easy, say yes! Tell them how thrilled you are. Indicate how much you appreciate the opportunity. End the conversation with plans for your next communication ("we'll be in touch once we've made your airline reservations", or "we'll contact you again a couple of weeks prior to the assignment"). It you are uncertain about the house sit tell them that you want to consider it and agree on a specific time that you will provide a response. If you have found that there is something objectionable, and you don't want the house sit, say so. Be honest. Both you and the homeowner can move on without taking up any more of each other's valuable time.

Promptly after the interview we suggest sending an e-mail to the owner thanking them for their consideration and, again, indicating your interest and willingness to provide any other information they might need.

If you are not selected for the assignment, don't take it personally. In fact, use the opportunity to re-connect via e-mail letting the homeowner know that you would be interested in some future date if they should need a sitter. We've not been selected for a house sit only to have the homeowner send us an e-mail a couple of days later and offer us one for another time. So, stay positive!

<u>Some additional considerations</u>

- Some homeowners may ask for a written agreement or, depending upon the circumstances, you may find one desirable. These can range from a simple letter to a multi-page agreement. There are examples of these agreements on most of the house sitting web sites for review. If this gives the homeowner another layer of security, and you find nothing objectionable in the agreement, then there is no reason not to sign it. Our belief is that the longer the assignment and the more complex the arrangements the better off both parties are by clarifying details with a written document.

- If you will be required to pay utilities or other expenses we recommend this be detailed in writing. If the costs are based on your usage you may need to read the meters upon your arrival and departure.

- If you are required to make a security deposit ask for a letter stating the terms under which that deposit will be refunded to you and the time frame in which that will occur after the house sit ends. Forms for this can be found on some of the websites and downloaded for your use.

You have the job (hurrah!)

In the following chapters we will discuss what you need to do to prepare for your house sitting assignment including some helpful tips regarding your travel preparations. We'll cover what information you will need in detail from the homeowner prior to their departure and the steps you need to take when your house sit ends to be sure you get invited back!

Chapter 8

BEFORE YOU GO AND ON THE ROAD

You may be doing a house sit for a night or for a year. You may only house sit once or twice a year as your vacation time allows or you may do as we did and give up your own home to house sit full-time. In this chapter we will discuss what preparations generally apply to all situations and then we'll delve into the details of preparing for life on the road as a full-time house sitter. If your interests are focused on short-term assignments only, we suggest you read the first section of the chapter and then skip to Chapter 9 where we address the steps to take upon your arrival.

As with any trip, you need to make your travel arrangements. If you are driving, it's simple. If you are flying, it can be a bit more of an issue if your house sitting assignment is several months away and you are uneasy spending the money for an airplane ticket months in advance. What happens if you or the homeowner has to cancel or change dates? At this point you need to decide if you want to purchase your ticket well in advance (which may cost less) or book closer to the date of the trip (which may cost more) when there is less time remaining for something to go wrong. If you purchase far in advance another option is buying a refundable ticket. We suggest you check the airline's website and read the fine print to determine the cost and restrictions applicable to changing the ticket you are considering. We usually book 2 months ahead if time allows, accepting that there are uncertainties in everything, knowing that we may have to pay to change our tickets if something unexpected occurs. We also know we may not get the best price buying our tickets only two months in advance if we are traveling in peak season for that particular location but it's a compromise we're comfortable with.

If you have questions about which airport is nearest your destination, the best way to get from the airport to the house, which bus route to take, or need driving directions, the best resource is the homeowner. Particularly in a foreign country, where you may not speak the language, learning how to get from point A to point B from a local is invaluable.

If you are traveling out of your home country to one requiring a passport check to see that yours is not near its expiration date. Many countries require that your passport be valid for 6 months beyond your date of travel.

Regarding your luggage we suggest you take only what you can comfortably manage on your own. There may not be resources to assist you with your luggage and you may have to be able to handle it by yourself. In some countries you may have to use stairs as elevators are not commonly available. Some streets you traverse may be cobblestone and not smooth pavement. Remember, you are staying in a private home and you will likely have a laundry facility at your disposal so you won't need as many clothing changes as you do when you are vacationing in a hotel. If you are traveling by plane check the airline's luggage size and weight restrictions and their carry-on policy.

Take clothes you will be comfortable in to do the tasks you will undertake and something nicer for the occasional dinner out. Take good walking shoes and whatever comfy shoes you like to wear around the house.

Be prepared for the weather and the bugs. A hat, sunscreen, insect repellant or umbrella can be your very best friends! Take some basic first aid supplies to have on hand. Don't assume that you will be able to find these items if you are going anywhere remote.

You might also add a small nightlight and flashlight to your bag. You are going to be in an unfamiliar place and nightlights can come in handy. If there is a power failure you may need a flashlight. Depending upon the country you are in you may need an electrical converter for any plug-in appliances.

If you are not going to have a car and are going to walk or depend upon public transportation it is handy to have a strong canvas bag with a good strap to carry groceries and other items. They pack flat and don't take up much room in the suitcase. We also use ours to tote the camera around rather than carrying our camera bag advertising that we are tourists. We each bring along small backpacks which we carry on the plane as our one allowed "personal" item. Their versatility makes them useful in many situations.

Leave your good jewelry at home and take inexpensive costume jewelry to wear. Also, consider replacing a camera strap that says "Canon" or "Nikon" with something plain that doesn't draw attention to your expensive camera. You don't want to make yourself a target for theft.

If you are traveling alone consider buying a small personal alarm that will clip to your handbag or belt. These high pitch alarms help draw attention if you need it and are inexpensive and available at most travel stores.

Have someplace that is secure to carry your passport, ATM and credit cards. We suggest traveling with two credit cards. If you are traveling as a couple, take different credit cards or cards with different account numbers. In the event one of you has your cards stolen, the other's cards will still be active. When we travel out of the country we always notify the credit card companies and our bank where we will be and the dates of our travel. Many now let you do this online. It lessens the likelihood of having a "hold" placed on your card for suspicious activity. But having said that, it still happens on occasion which is another reason why we travel with two cards each. Write down your ATM and credit card numbers and the domestic and/or international customer service numbers and keep the information separate from your cards. Also make a copy of your passport and put it somewhere separate from the actual passport. If your originals are stolen having the credit card information and a copy of your passport makes it much easier than scrambling after the fact. We've also found that American

Express cards are not accepted in many small establishments so make at least one of your cards a Visa or MasterCard.

Either purchase foreign funds through your bank prior to leaving or enough at the airport upon arrival to get you through the first day or two. You will likely get a better exchange rate from a bank so we don't recommend purchasing any more than that at the airport. If you are traveling with a partner split up the cash between the two of you. If one of you is pick-pocketed you will still have cash for a taxi ride to the bank or ATM.

Take a travel guide if you think you will have time to see any of the sites. They are downloadable on Kindle and Nook if space is a concern. If you don't take a guide get a map either before you go or when you arrive. In popular tourist spots they are usually available for free.

If you plan to use your phone out of the country check with your carrier for rates and rate plans. If you have a smart phone you will likely need to upgrade your plan through your carrier or turn your data roaming off. Data roaming outside of your home country can be prohibitively expensive and, if you forget to turn it off, you could end up with a costly surprise when you receive your next billing. Some phones have removable SIM cards and you can purchase one usable in the country you are visiting and buy minutes. Some phones are locked. Check online with your phone's manufacturer for your specific model. Another option is buying an inexpensive phone and some minutes in the country you are visiting.

Learn at least a few words of the local language. Being able to say "hello", "please", "thank-you" and "help" are the bare minimum. We frequently use Google's online translator when we travel — it is a wonderful tool and very simple to use. It can be accessed at www.translate.google.com. If you like, get a hand-held electronic translator to carry with you.

<u>Living on the road</u>

You may have thought about doing this for years and have a good grasp on all of the details that will come into play with this type of a lifestyle change. However, if you haven't, we'd like to share with you some of the items that we did in preparation for our life on the road. The list is by no means all-inclusive as your situation may demand other considerations. There are entire books written on this subject that go into great detail. But having had the experience we can at least give you some food for thought and some encouragement! We've arranged these suggestions loosely by the time in advance you may want to consider doing them. Each person's needs are different so adjust the timing to your situation.

6 Months before you plan to leave (or longer if you plan to sell your home):

- Decide what you will do with your own home. If you are a renter, you can give up your place or sublet it as allowed by your rental agreement. If you own your home, you could sell it, rent it or leave it empty. The latter is probably the least desirable for security and maintenance issues. If you rent it, will you be able to meet your commitments as a landlord while you are living on the road? We opted for using a management company that would interview and screen tenants, process the legal paperwork required, arrange maintenance as needed, collect the rent, and conduct eviction proceedings if a tenant needed to be removed from the property. In our area, the fee for this service ranges from 8 – 10% of the monthly rent. If you go this route, we suggest you ask people you know for referrals and speak with a few companies before you decide which to hire. You should also contact your homeowner's insurance carrier to notify them of any changes you make.

3 months before you plan to leave:

- Decide what you will do with your belongings. Will they need to be stored, sold or given away – maybe a combination of all three options? Many people find this a liberating experience while others have real difficulty in parting with even the most minor of possessions. Do what feels comfortable. Conduct a garage sale or contact a charity to donate items you no longer want. Research moving companies, fees and schedule your movers as needed. Shop around for a storage unit if you plan to store your belongings. While this may seem premature, we found that in our area, the larger units had waiting lists.

- Sit down and make a list of everything you can think of that you must pay for over the course of a year. Look at past checking and credit card statements. Most of the "business of life" has some monetary aspect to it so these statements provide a good accounting of not only your financial responsibilities, but will also jog your memory about that random item that you address one time a year.

Create four categories on your list – monthly, quarterly, annually, and randomly and post your entries accordingly. Which of these responsibilities will be ongoing and which will cease when you begin life on the road? How will you address them? Can you pay your bills online through your bank's bill paying system or will you need to make other accommodations? Check websites for items in question. It is possible to set up access and payment processes for just about everything. Go "paperless" and begin receiving statements and notifications online now as it can take more than one billing cycle to implement. As a reminder, we activated the "alerts" option on the various company websites providing us with advance reminders when a bill was coming due.

- After you have determined the action you will need to take for each item on the list, transfer the items that require action to another list – only this time by the timeframe in which you will address them prior to your departure. We suggest 90, 60, 30 days, 2 weeks and 1 week. As other tasks occur to you, add them to these "time frame" lists. You will feel less overwhelmed and be less likely to forget something if you are organized.

- Make a master user name and password list. This list should be as complete as you can make it. Add the account numbers, web site addresses, telephone numbers, due dates, renewal dates, and whatever other information is needed for full access to your accounts. We recommend that you install a securely encrypted program on your laptop where you can store this data. We use Keypass, but there are many others available. For backup, enter the same information on a thumb drive to keep in a separate location from your computer should it be stolen. The thumb-drive should also be used if you access your accounts through a computer that is not your own. This will avoid leaving a "ghost" of data that could possibly be obtained by someone else. We suggest that you not carry a paper copy of your information with you because should it fall into the wrong hands, you could potentially spend months cleaning up the mess. However, if you decide to do so, consider keeping the user names separate from the passwords – using two lists which are kept separately. At least that way, both items must be obtained to be of any use. Give a paper copy of your passwords to someone that you trust. In the event that you lose everything while traveling, they can fax you a copy so you can notify and cancel accounts as needed.

- Make arrangements to cut down on your paper mail as much as possible by canceling subscriptions and memberships that you will not need while on the road. Call the companies that routinely send you catalogs and ask to be removed from their mailing list. Arrange to have your mail forwarded to a good friend or family member. Hopefully, they will have little mail to attend to if you have taken all of the steps outlined above. You will need periodic communication with this person either by phone or Internet to keep apprised of anything that requires your attention. If you do not have a friend or family member willing to do this for you, another alternative is renting a mailbox from a mail service. Many of these services will forward mail upon request if you are somewhere with mail delivery. If you will be unable to receive mail, ask if they will periodically open the mail and review it with you over the phone.

- Arrange for the storage or sale of your vehicles if you will not be using them. If you keep your vehicle, remember to note when your registration and insurance payments will come due and verify that you can pay them on-line. Some

States allow for "non-operational" status with reduced registration fees. Contact your insurance agent to advise them if your vehicle will be in storage.

- Update your will if needed and store it in a safe deposit box along with any other important documents.

- Advise your accountant, lawyer, financial planner, and anyone else that assists you in the "business of life" of your plans. Discuss with your accountant your options for tax preparation.

- Schedule appointments with your doctor and dentist. Have your routine annual exams. Obtain copies of any medical records you may need while you travel. Have vaccinations that may be needed for the countries you plan to visit.

- If you wear glasses, have your prescription updated and obtain a spare pair to take with you or a copy of your prescription.

- If you take prescription medications you will need to develop a plan to obtain them wherever you are going to be. This can be a bit of a hassle depending upon your location and your insurance situation as some plans will not fill prescriptions for more than 90 days at a time and most don't offer coverage out of the country. You may need to see a doctor on the road if this is the case.

- Spend a couple of hours on the Internet looking at medical evacuation insurance and international health insurance policies if your medical coverage does not extend outside your home country. Many countries provide excellent medical care that is more affordable than the U.S., so paying out of pocket for routine care may be your best option. However, depending upon where you are going, you may be more comfortable with an air evacuation policy for emergency situations – only you can decide upon that. A good site to begin your search is www.insuremytrip.com. The site offers comparisons on a variety of types of travel related insurance.

30 days before you plan to leave:

- Update your address and phone lists and put that information on your computer and your thumb drive.
- Install Skype so you can do video calls with your family and friends. It works well and it is free. (www.Skype.com)
- Decide which clothes you will take with you. Remember you should be able to carry whatever it is you decide to take.

- Purchase a laptop and a travel case if you do not already own them.

- Check your cell phone plan and make changes as needed.

- Go through your file cabinet and shred old paperwork, minimizing what you need to store.

- Tell all of your friends and family, if they don't already know of your plans, what you are doing. Set up a blog, website or Facebook page to stay in touch with people while you are on the road.

2-3 weeks before you plan to leave:

- Make arrangements to turn off your utilities and other services.

- Arrange for carpet cleaning, window washing, etc. if you are responsible for that prior to vacating your current residence.

- Order any foreign currency from your bank.

- Contact your bank and credit card companies to inform them of your travel plans. Cancel any credit cards that you will not be using.

- Pack your belongings if you will be doing this yourself. If you will be storing your belongings, set aside and mark any boxes that you want stored near the front of the unit for ease of access. For example, we have a wardrobe with seasonal changes of clothing and our paperwork and tax returns at the front of our storage unit so those items are readily accessible should we need any of them.

- Load your favorite music onto your I-pod and books onto your e-reader or computer. Check your camera battery and supply of memory cards.

One week before you leave:

- Pack the items that you will take with you. Do this now so that you know what is going to fit and what you may have to leave behind. If you will be flying, weigh your suitcases to make certain that they do not exceed the airlines weight restrictions. Pack liquids according to the most recent security rules.
- Put together a list of important information, such as the bank you use, your attorney's name, the location of your storage unit and vehicles, and give it to a family member or friend for use in the event that something unforeseen occurs.

As you can see, there are many items to address prior to leaving and, depending upon your situation, can take months of preparation.

In addition to the practical considerations, we suggest you give some thought to those things in life that enhance your emotional well-being. In your life on the road as a house sitter, what is it that will make you feel at home in each place you stay? For us, it is having music and books that we enjoy. We take our I-pod with us and a very small lightweight speaker dock. We have our Kindles loaded with books. We each have a lap top computer to work on our digital photos, write on our blog, research house sitting and travel opportunities, and Skype with family and friends. These things give us that bit of "home" that we want with us. What will do that for you?

Another consideration when living on the road is your physical well-being. Travel can be a challenge to maintaining your diet and exercise program.   We walk a lot and have a routine using exercise bands for resistance training that we do regularly. The bands are lightweight, can be used anywhere, and take up minimal space in our luggage. A short-term gym membership for weight training may be an option in your location or you may be able to pay on a per class basis for yoga, Pilates, Zumba, spinning, etc. Be creative in coming up with ways to stay fit.

If you are particular in your eating habits, you may have to adjust to living without certain foods you normally eat. Learning about the local cuisine and trying some of those ingredients you've never seen before are part of the adventure. We loaded a few of our favorite recipes on our computer and when we have access to the necessary ingredients, we occasionally make ourselves some "comfort" food.

There is no doubt that living on the road is a grand adventure. But even the hardiest of travelers have moments of home-sickness, so take some time in advance of leaving and think of ways that you can make yourself feel at home on the road.

We're often asked what we do "in between" house sitting assignments since we are full time house sitters and no longer have our own home to go to. While we do our best to book as much time house sitting as we can we sometimes end up with a few days (and sometimes even a few weeks) in between our assignments. We use this time to visit our families and friends, we book short-term vacation rentals just to take a break and recharge ourselves, or we take the opportunity for our own vacation and do some traveling. Often, we take advantage of the time to explore and travel somewhere near to our next house sitting assignment to minimize our travel expenses and maximize our opportunities. For instance, we did a house sit in the Yucatan, but we took time beforehand to visit the ruins in Tulum and the surrounding area. This is one of the real advantages of house sitting!

House sitting is fun and rewarding in many ways, but it is also a big responsibility and it can sometimes be challenging work so we enjoy having these breaks and try to make the most of them.

Chapter 9

YOUR FIRST ASSIGNMENT

Here you are, you've arrived at your first house sitting assignment and you are getting to know the homeowner, their home, their pets and their expectations. It can be a bit overwhelming at first. You may have only a couple of hours with the homeowner to learn the routine. It depends. Some homeowners will ask you to come a day or two in advance of their departure so they can take you on their dog's normal walk, show you where the nearest market is, introduce you to some friends or neighbors. Whatever the situation, you have a lot of ground to cover before the homeowner departs and entrusts their home and pets to your care.

Your homeowner may have had experience with house sitters before and be well versed as to what information they need to provide. Some homeowners have given us written information about their house and their pet's care, maps for the area, restaurant recommendations, bus schedules, lists of friends to contact for assistance, etc. If the homeowner is well prepared your orientation will go smoothly. For other homeowners this might be their first experience using a house sitter or they may be more focused on last minute details with their jobs or vacation plans and not as well prepared as you would like. If that is the case, it will fall upon you to take the lead and get the information you need before they walk out the door.

We've developed a list of items that we refer to during our orientation to the home and pets we're going to be caring for. We've found it helps keep us focused and prevents our overlooking anything we might need to know. Not all of the items listed apply to every house sitting situation, so don't be overwhelmed. We'll go over it here, and we've included it at the end of this manual in a format that you can copy for your own use.

<u>Household care information</u>

- Locations of emergency shut-offs for gas and water lines
- If propane is used, location of tank and delivery service information
- Solar heating and/or back-up generator location and operating instructions
- Location garbage is stored, days of pick-up service and details on recycling and any required sorting

- Operation of stoves and ovens, regular and on-demand hot water heaters, water purification system, heating and cooling systems and thermostat operating instructions
- Drinking water — if bottled, how and when it is delivered?
- If housekeepers, gardeners, pool or spa maintenance personnel are used, their schedule, general outline of their duties and how they are to be paid
- If you are to maintain the pool, the location of supplies and instructions on their use and the frequency needed
- Watering instructions for potted plants and yard
- Location and operation of lawn mower and/or gardening tools if you are expected to cut the grass, weed, etc.
- Location of vacuum cleaner, extra bags, cleaning supplies
- Remote control for garage door
- Are there any restrictions with on-street parking?
- Operating instructions and codes for alarm systems
- Internet operating instructions and wireless access code
- Instructions for television remote controls
- Instructions for mail pick-up and answering phone calls
- Do the neighbors know that there will be a house sitter occupying the home?
- Are there friends nearby to help if you need assistance?

- Locations of nearest grocery store, bank or ATM, hospital or 24 hour clinic, and pharmacy
- If you are in a foreign country, is there the equivalent of a 911 emergency number?
- What is the homeowner's policy regarding visitors while the home is in your care?

Pet care information

- Names and ages of each of the pets
- Description of the general daily habits of each pet and any issue a particular pet may have (Do all the pets get along?)
- Feeding instructions, special dietary requirements
- Location of pet food and where to purchase additional food
- Medications to administer, frequency and dosage
- Exercise routine, frequency and location of walks, dog parks
- Location of pet carriers, pet beds, pet toys
- Local pet leash and litter laws, bags for pet poop
- Instructions for disposal of cat litter and pet poop
- Bathing instructions
- Veterinarian's name, phone number and location
- Location of nearest 24 hour pet emergency clinic

- Procedure for transporting pet in an emergency (is the use of the owner's vehicle authorized?)

While we're on the subject of pet care, we believe the best way to help pets adjust to their owner's absence is to maintain their normal routine and give them reassurance with kind words and lots of love and attention.

Occasionally, a pet will have problems adjusting to your presence. We recommend patience and giving them time to develop a sense of trust. Don't force your attention upon them or invade their space. They will accept you when they are ready. In the meantime, maintain their routine as much as possible and remember that this is their home and you are the guest.

One situation that we hope to never face is one in which a pet has had an accident or health problem that is life threatening. Fortunately, most homeowners are readily available by cell phone should such an unfortunate situation occur and decisions regarding their pet's care are immediately required. In the event that your homeowner is going to be unavailable to you, we suggest you ask the difficult question of what their wishes are for their pet's care in a life threatening circumstance.

On a lighter note, we've found pet care to be one of the most pleasurable aspects of house sitting. In fact, the most difficult part of caring for pets can be when your house sit comes to an end and you have to say good-bye to your new friends!

There are many details to taking care of someone's home and animals. The more you know, the better prepared you will be. Each situation is unique, but having the list as a starting point to address the basics is helpful.

Longer-term house sits

Certainly all of the things we've covered up to this point are applicable to you as a long-term house sitter. But taking care of someone's home for a lengthy period can involve more tasks and more maintenance. Here are some considerations for the longer- term assignment:

- Your homeowner may have prepaid the household bills or you may be tasked to do so on their behalf. If they have given you cash to cover these expenses keep a written log of how you disburse the money. If you are expected to expend your own funds, with the understanding that you will receive reimbursement upon the homeowner's return, you should have a written agreement in addition to keeping a log of disbursements. If the homeowner has prepaid the utilities, phone, Internet, etc., please ask that they have copies of those receipts set aside for you to substantiate payment should some problem arise. Although the service was prepaid, we had our garbage service cut off while house sitting in a foreign country. Having that receipt marked "paid" came in handy.

• If there are pets involved, long-term care could include trips to the veterinarian or groomer. How will you transport the pet(s)? Are pet carriers available? Bathing, flea treatments, periodic treatments such as heartworm medications, etc. may need to be administered.

• Seasonal work at the home may need to be addressed. That field behind the house that barely grows in winter will be a fire hazard in the spring without some serious weed whacking. Do the rain gutters need leaves cleaned out at the end of fall before the winter rains come? Talk to the homeowner about the seasonal or periodic maintenance tasks required and who will be responsible for them.

• The longer the house sitting assignment, the more maintenance issues that can arise with a home. Ask the homeowner to make a list of their preferred service companies. If the homeowner is not going to be readily available by phone or Internet you should agree to a monetary limit on what you are authorized to spend, and expect reimbursement for, in the event you need to repair or replace an item that is important to the running of the house and to your comfort. For example, if the hot water heater goes out, you cannot be expected to tough it out. If the dishwasher goes on the fritz, it's an inconvenience but perhaps not something you can't do without.

- Ask the homeowner to give you a few contact names of friends nearby who could give you a hand in an emergency or provide assistance should some unforeseen issue arise. This is particularly useful in a country where you do not speak the language.

- You and the homeowner should discuss and agree to a notification period that will be given should either of you need to end this long term arrangement sooner than anticipated.

Your homeowner may be half a world away, but readily accessible by phone or Internet should you need their authorization or advice to address an issue. That's the ideal situation. However, if the homeowner will be unreachable for periods of time, more advance planning is needed. Both you and the homeowner need to feel confident in your arrangement.

What about the "what if's...?"

The most common questions people ask us when they learn we are house sitters will begin with the words "what if...." What if the house isn't what you expected? What if the house is really dirty? What if the dog is hard to handle? What if something happens with your own family while you are housesitting – if someone gets sick or there is a death in the family? What if the neighborhood seems sketchy? What if the homeowner asks you to do something extra around the house that you hadn't previously agreed to?

Let's face it, you cannot plan for every eventuality in life nor can you do so with house sitting. However, we offer the following suggestions to help guide you through that dreaded "what if..." situation.

- <u>Advance preparation</u> – follow the steps outlined in the interview process to gain as much insight as possible beforehand. Don't make assumptions – do your homework and your research to minimize the possibilities of a misunderstanding or disappointing situation occurring in the first place. Ask for clarification when you don't fully understand a situation or expectation. Conduct your interview or a follow-up conversation either in-person or via Skype. Being "face-to-face" with someone is telling. Do they look you in the eye during the interview? Do they avoid directly answering questions or seem vague on the details? Do you mesh with this person or do your personalities seem to clash? Your instincts are an invaluable guide so listen to them.

- <u>Once you have arrived</u> – there is likely to be something about most house sits that isn't "perfect" but if you can live with it then do so. However, if it is something truly objectionable address it immediately with the *ultimate goal of achieving resolution*. The best way to do this is to offer a solution that you and the homeowner can agree to which will render the situation acceptable. For instance, if the house is filthy, suggest to the homeowner that they pay for a professional cleaning before they leave. If a pet frightens you and you cannot control it, you could suggest creating a confined space or kenneling. Whatever the problem, try to reach a workable solution. If you can't then you may have to tell the homeowner you cannot follow through with the house sitting arrangement as it is. You are there to honor your commitment to them, but they must also honor their commitment to you. If the homeowner suddenly asks you to do more than was previously agreed to, you will need to decide if you can accommodate their request. If at all possible, do so. You want to build good will and a solid reputation as a professional house sitter. If you cannot do what is asked, explain that whatever it may be wasn't part of your original commitment to them and that you are not comfortable undertaking this new task or expectation.

- <u>A personal emergency occurs during your house sit</u> — you will need to contact the homeowner to explain the seriousness of the situation and, if possible, offer alternatives. For instance, if you can attend to the emergency and return then perhaps a friend of the homeowner, a neighbor, or a local pet sitter can come to the home in your absence to care for the animals, pick up the mail, etc. If you are a couple, perhaps one can stay while one travels home. If you can't return to fulfill your obligation then the homeowner may opt to find another house sitter, leave the home unattended, or they may need to return themselves. This type of situation is difficult and stressful for everyone involved so do what you can to assist the homeowner.

Chapter 10

PREPARING FOR THE HOMEOWNER'S RETURN

You've come to the end of your house sit and now it's time to prepare for the homeowner's return and your departure. Your goal now is to end this adventure on a good note and, if you like, set yourself up to be invited back at some future date. We've put together our suggestions here and you will find them in checklist form at the back of the book to copy for your own use. We will begin with the basics of putting the house in order and move on to some suggestions for making the homeowner's welcome home a warm one. We recommend you begin preparations a few days in advance of the homeowner's return.

Getting the house ready:

- Remove any old food and "leftover" items from the refrigerator and wipe down the shelves and sidewalls. If you have unused foodstuffs that you believe the homeowner can use, leave them. Do the same for the pantry items.
- Wash all of your dishes and put them away.
- Clean kitchen sink, countertops and stovetop.

- If the kitchen scrubber sponge is old, buy a new one and set it out.
- Wash kitchen and bath towels.
- Wash beds sheets and remake the bed.
- Remove used bars of soap from the bathroom and replace with fresh bars.
- Clean the bathroom toilet, sink and mirrors. Set out fresh towels.
- Sweep or vacuum the house and dust.
- Remove garbage from all waste bins and put in new bags.
- Wash pet bedding, water and food bowls as needed.
- Water plants, put away garden tools, and neaten patio areas.
- If you have used the homeowner's vehicle, take it to the car wash and fill the gas tank to the level it was when they left.
- Organize any paperwork that you have kept for expense tracking, mail, records of phone calls, etc.
- Leave the homeowner with the same amount of supplies that you were left with – toilet paper, paper towels, garbage bags, napkins, Kleenex, plastic and foil wrap, plastic bags, cooking oils, salad dressings, spices, etc. Whatever you have used – replace it.

- If you've moved anything, put it back in its original location. You want the homeowner to feel like they have never left, not like they are coming back to a different house!
- Do a final inspection of the home and check that you have not left behind any of your personal items.
- If using the homeowner's safe, remove your belongings.
- If you have made new friends during your house sit, be certain to update your phone and address list with their contact information.

In addition to the basic tasks, we suggest you put some extra effort in to make the homeowner's return easy and pleasurable. It's thoughtful to provide some staple items like eggs, bread, milk, and coffee so the homeowner won't have to go to the grocery store immediately upon their return. If you cook, consider leaving a simple, home cooked meal pre-prepared in the refrigerator. Some pasta and sauce, a cold chicken or even some sandwich making items will be appreciated.

We usually buy some fresh flowers and set them out. If your homeowner likes wine, considering leaving a nice bottle for them. If not, maybe a box of chocolates or a bowl of fresh fruit. Some house sitters leave thank-you cards. Some simple gesture that indicates your appreciation is all that is needed.

Before you depart, discuss any remaining business with the homeowner. If you have a deposit that needs returned, or you made any expenditures from their funds or yours, review the disbursement documentation with them and finalize your business.

Be certain to express your thanks for their having selected you to be their house sitter. If they are happy with your service, ask if they will act as a reference for you and e-mail you a brief letter once they get settled in. If you would like to house sit for them again, say so. Tell them that you would appreciate a referral to any of their friends or family members and leave them a couple of your business cards. You don't want to be pushy, but if you want their future business you should ask for it.

Then, take your leave. Wish them well, say good-bye, but don't linger too long. Sometimes, particularly with long-term house sits, it can be a bit difficult to leave the home you have so diligently cared for and pets that you have grown fond of, but leave you must!

In closing

Congratulations — you've just learned everything you need to know to become a successful house sitter. We appreciate that you have allowed us to share our experience and suggestions with you. We hope this book has been helpful and given you a sense of confidence and a willingness to explore our big beautiful world through the adventure of house sitting.

We wish you all the best in your adventures traveling the world one house at a time!

Colleen & Rick

P.S. We welcome any comments and are happy to answer any questions that you may have. We can be reached via e-mail at casaray513@att.net.

HOUSE SITTING CONTACT LOG

Application date: _____ Website source: _____

Sitting Dates: _____ Location: _____

H.O. Name: _____ E-mail: _____

Skype Name: _____ Phone: _____

Details: _____

Pet Info: _____

References sent _____ Police Check _____ Other: _____

Application date: _____ Website source: _____

Sitting Dates: _____ Location: _____

H.O. Name: _____ E-mail: _____

Skype Name: _____ Phone: _____

Details: _____

Pet Info: _____

References sent _____ Police Check _____ Other: _____

Application date: _____ Website source: _____

Sitting Dates: _____ Location: _____

H.O. Name: _____ E-mail: _____

Skype Name: _____ Phone: _____

Details: _____

Pet Info: _____

References sent _____ Police Check _____ Other: _____

ARRIVAL CHECK LIST

Homeowner contact information _____

_____

Locations of emergency shut-offs for gas and water lines

_____

Propane tank location and delivery service information

_____

Solar heating and generator location and operation instructions

_____

Location garbage is stored and days of pick-up service, recycling details

_____

Operation of stoves and ovens, regular and on-demand hot water heaters, water purification, heating and cooling systems

_____

Drinking water – if bottled, delivery schedule and source

_____

Housekeepers, gardeners, pool or spa maintenance worker details and payments

_____

Pool supplies and instructions on their use and frequency needed

_____

Watering instructions for potted plants and yard

_____

Location and operation of lawn mower and/or gardening tools

_____

Location of vacuum cleaner, extra bags, cleaning supplies

_____

Remote control for garage door opener

_____

Parking restrictions in effect

_____

Operating instructions and codes for alarm systems

_____

Internet operating instructions and wireless access code

_____

Television remote controls and operating instructions

_____

Mail pick-up and phone call instructions

_____

Neighbor notification of house sit

_____

Nearby friends for assistance

_____

Nearest grocery store, bank, ATM, hospital or 24 hour clinic, and pharmacy locations

_____

_____

Foreign country, 911 emergency number   _____

Homeowner's visitor policy

_____

PET CARE INFORMATION

Names and ages of each pet

_____

Description of the general daily habits and behaviors

_____

Feeding instructions, special dietary requirements

_____

Location of pet food and where to purchase additional food

_____

Medications to administer, frequency and dosage

_____

Exercise routine, frequency and location of walks, dog park locations

_____

Location of pet carriers, pet beds, pet toys

_____

Local pet leash and litter laws, bags for pet poop, disposal instructions

_____

Bathing instructions

_____

Veterinarian's name, phone number and location and nearest 24-hour emergency clinic

_____

Emergency transportation instructions

_____

DEPARTURE CHECKLIST

- Remove any old food and "leftover" items from the refrigerator and wipe down the shelves and sidewalls. If you have unused foodstuffs that you believe the homeowner can use, leave them. Do the same for the pantry items
- Wash all of your dishes and put them away
- Clean kitchen sink, wipe down countertops and stovetop
- Replace kitchen scrubber sponge
- Wash kitchen and bath towels
- Wash beds sheets and remake the bed
- Remove used bars of soap from the bathroom and replace with fresh bars
- Clean the bathroom toilet, sink and mirrors and put out fresh towels
- Sweep or vacuum the house and dust
- Remove garbage from all waste bins and put in new bags
- Wash pet bedding, water and food bowls
- Water plants, put away garden tools, and neaten patio areas
- If you used the homeowner's vehicle, wash it and fill the gas tank to the level it was when they left.
- Organize any paperwork that you have kept for expense tracking, mail, records of phone calls, etc.
- Replace any supplies that you have used: toilet paper, paper towels, garbage bags, napkins, Kleenex, plastic and foil wrap, plastic bags, cooking oils, salad dressings, spices, etc.
- If you've moved anything, put it back in its original location
- Double check that you have not left any of your personal items behind
- If using the homeowner's safe, remove your belongings
- Walk through the home and do a final inspection